SHRIMAT BHAGAVATAM

INSHORT OF GITA

NIVRUTHI SHEKAR

Copyright © Nivruthi Shekar
All Rights Reserved.

This book has been published with all efforts taken to make the material error-free after the consent of the author. However, the author and the publisher do not assume and hereby disclaim any liability to any party for any loss, damage, or disruption caused by errors or omissions, whether such errors or omissions result from negligence, accident, or any other cause.

While every effort has been made to avoid any mistake or omission, this publication is being sold on the condition and understanding that neither the author nor the publishers or printers would be liable in any manner to any person by reason of any mistake or omission in this publication or for any action taken or omitted to be taken or advice rendered or accepted on the basis of this work. For any defect in printing or binding the publishers will be liable only to replace the defective copy by another copy of this work then available.

"You opened the doors to the world for me and showed me
how to go through them,

Staying beside to make sure I'm making it through,

This one is because of you".

- A

Contents

Contents

Preface

The Bhagavad Gita is one of the most widely read religious texts today. It influences people's lives all across the world. The Srimad Bhagavad Gita is a Mahabharata conversation between Lord Krishna and Arjuna that is told in the Bhishma Parva. The Bhagavad Gita is divided into eighteen chapters, with a total of 701 Sanskrit lines. Within these verses, a significant amount of information has been compacted. Sri Krishna imparted profound, magnificent, and soul-stirring spiritual truths and explained the scarce insights of Yoga, Vedanta, Bhakti, and Karma during His most instructional and engaging conversation with Arjuna on the battlefield of Kurukshetra. Bhagavan Vyasa afterwards documented all of Lord Krishna's teachings as the Song Celestial or Srimad Bhagavad Gita for the benefit of all humanity. Bhagavan Vyasa owes humanity a profound debt of gratitude for presenting this Celestial Song to humanity for guidance in daily life, spiritual upliftment, and Self-realization. The Gita, which is the science of the Soul, can be fully utilised by those who are self-controlled and have trust. One should read at least one discourse from the scripture every day to keep its important lessons fresh in our minds. Each discourse is preceded by a brief summary that summarises the content of that discourse.

Essence Of Gita

The Gita repeatedly emphasises the importance of cultivating a non-attachment or detachment attitude. It continuously encourages people to exist in a world like water on a lotus petal. "As a lotus petal is not polluted by water, he who does deeds, surrendering them to Brahman and renouncing attachment, is not polluted by sin." Infatuation causes attachment. It is the descendent of Rajas' qualities. Sattwa is the source of detachment. The first is a demonic quality, whereas the latter is heavenly. Attachment is the result of ignorance, selfishness, and passion, and it leads to death; detachment is the result of wisdom, and it leads to liberation. Detachment is a difficult discipline to master. You may stumble like a toddler attempting to walk, but you must get back up with a smile on your face. Failures are stepping stones to success, not stumbling obstacles.

Always try to stay in touch with your inner self. Stay in your centre. Constantly think of yourself. After then, all attachments will immediately die.The Lord's attachment is a powerful antidote to all worldly attachments. Because his love is pure and heavenly, he who has no attachments can truly love others. "Therefore, always execute activity that should be done without attachment; for man approaches the Supreme by doing deed without attachment."

Prayer To Vyasa

"Namostu te vyaasa visaalabuddhe"

"phullaaravindaa yatapatranetra"

"Yena twayaa bhaaratatailapoornah"

"prajwaalito jnaanamayah pradeepah"

Salutations to you, O Vyasa, of vast intellect and huge eyes like the petals of a full-fledged lotus, by whom the lantern of heavenly wisdom, filled with Mahabharata has been lighted.

Prayer To The Guru

"Gururbrahmaa gururvishnur"

"gururdevo maheshwarah;"

"Guruh saakshaat param brahma"

"tasmai shree gurave namah"

Guru is the creator (Brahma); Guru is the preserver (Vishnu); Guru is the destroyer (Maheshvara); Guru is verily the Supreme Absolute. To that Guru we prostrate.

THE BEGINNING

CHAPTER ONE

INTRODUCTION

Pandu and Dhritarashtra were brothers. Pandu married Kunti and Madri, while Dhritarashtra wedded Gandhari. King Pandu was punished for committing a mistake while poaching, preventing him from reuniting with his wife. Kunti received a blessing for her true devotion to a wise sage when she was younger, and she had three offspring from Yama, Vayu, and Indra, namely Yudhisthira, Bhima, and Arjuna. Through the celestial medics known as Asvini-Devatas, Madri had twins, Nakula and Sahadeva. Dhritarashtra and his wife Gandhari had a total of 111 children. Dhritarashtra raised Pandu's sons, the Pandavas, as well as his other sons, the Kauravas after Pandu died.

The Pandavas and Kauravas were born and raised together, but the Kauravas couldn't stand them because of their bravery and cleverness. As a result, the Pandavas agreed to split up their kingdom in half and live separately. Duryodhana, the Kauravas' king, was enraged by the Pandavas' pomp, wealth, and glory during the Rajasuya Yajna, and summoned Yudhisthira to a round of dice, where he falsely defeated him, losing all of his worldly assets, including Draupadi. Finally, it was decided that the Pandavas, including Draupadi, would spend twelve years in exile in the forest, following which they would have to live in secret for another year, undetected by the Kauravas.

After completing the thirteen years of exile, which included many hurdles and dangers posed by the Kauravas, the Pandavas sought the Kauravas for their portion of the kingdom, as per the conditions of the agreement. Duryodhana, on the other hand, categorically refused to give up as much land as a needle could cover. The Pandavas chose to go to battle, following Mother Kunti's advice and Lord Krishna's inspiration, to demonstrate their rightful claim to the kingdom by defeating the Kauravas.

Duryodhana and Arjuna, representing the Kauravas and Pandavas, were despatched to Dwaraka to seek the support of Lord Krishna, the Yadava hero, in the fight. Krishna was found sleeping on a mattress in His palace by both of them. Duryodhana entered the room and went to sit at the top of the couch, while Arjuna sat near the Lord's feet. Sri Krishna initially saw Arjuna and then Duryodhana sitting on a bench when He first opened His eyes. Sri Krishna, after inquiring about their well-being and the reason for their visit, gave Arjuna priority, as was customary, due to his age and also because He saw Arjuna first. Arjuna was challenged to choose between Krishna, who was unarmed, and His strong army, the Narayani Sena. Arjuna, a follower of Sri Krishna, voiced his intention to have the Lord accompany him, ignoring the mighty Narayani Sena, despite Krishna's warning that He would stay a spectator, bound by the vow of not fighting or taking up arms. Duryodhana stated his desire for a formidable army to assist his army in the war, believing Arjuna to be dumb.

"O, Lord!" Arjuna exclaimed when Krishna questioned why he picked Him instead of taking up arms. You can destroy all forces simply by looking at them. So why should

I choose that useless army? I've had a long-held yearning in my heart for you to be my charioteer. Please grant my request in this conflict." The Divine, who is always the most ardent lover of His disciples, gladly approved his request, and thus He became Arjuna's charioteer in the Mahabharata fight.

After Duryodhana and Arjuna returned from Dwaraka, Lord Krishna went to Hastinapura as the Pandavas' emissary and attempted to halt the war. However, the egoistic Duryodhana, led by Sakuni, refused to cooperate with the peacekeeping mission and attempted to confine Lord Krishna, at which time Krishna revealed His Absolute Form (Viswarupa). By the Lord's Grace, even the blind Dhritarashtra saw it. Due to his affection for his sons, King Dhritarashtra was unable to manage them, and the Kaurava chief, Duryodhana, resolved to fight the strong Pandavas in vain.

"If you desire to see this horrible slaughter with your own eyes, I may give you the power of vision," the sage Veda Vyasa remarked to blind Dhritarashtra as both sides prepared to begin the battle. "O Chief of the Brahmarishis!" the Kaurava king answered. I have no wish to witness the death of my family with my own eyes, but I would like to know all of the specifics of the war."The sage then bestowed divine sight on Sanjaya, the king's trusted adviser, and told him, "Sanjaya will explain to you all the occurrences of the conflict." He will see, hear, or otherwise learn about everything that happens during the conflict. Whether an incident occurs in front of his sight or over his back, amid the day or night, privately or publicly, and whether it is turned into real action or merely appears in his mind, it will not escape his notice. Everything will be shown to him as it occurs. He will not get tired or be touched by any weapon.

After 10 days of fighting between Pandavas and the Kauravas, Sanjaya informs Dhritarashtra that the mighty warrior Bhishma has been hurled from his chariot by Arjuna. In anguish, the monarch orders Sanjaya to recount the entire ten-day conflict, beginning at the beginning and ending exactly as it happened. The Bhagavad Gita emerges here.

I THE YOGA OF THE DESPONDENCY OF ARJUNA

CHAPTER TWO

FIRST DISCLOSURE

On the holy plain of Kurukshetra, the great Mahabharata war between the Pandavas and the Kauravas took place. Following the failure of Lord Krishna's peace mission, when He Himself went to Hastinapura as the Pandavas' emissary, the Pandavas had no choice but to fight for their rightful share of the kingdom.On the battlefield, all of the famous warriors from both sides had gathered. The vast plain was covered in tents and waggons, weapons and machines, chariots and animals.

In a magnificent chariot drawn by white horses, Lord Krishna arrived on the scene. He was to serve as Arjuna's charioteer, one of the Pandava princes. The sound of hundreds of conches suddenly blaring announced the start of the battle. Arjuna blew the "Devadatta" conch, while his brother, Bhima, blew the "Paundra." All of the other great warriors blew their conches as well.

As the two armies prepared to fight, Arjuna requested that Krishna place his chariot between them so that he could survey his foes. He was perplexed by the scene in front of him, which included fathers and grandfathers, teachers and uncles, fathers-in-law, grandsons, relatives, and comrades on both sides. Arjuna's mind was a jumble of thoughts. Should he take part in this heinous crime? Was it right to murder one's relatives in the name of a kingdom and a few pleasures? Wouldn't it be preferable for him to hand over everything to his enemies and retire in peace? Arjuna was overcome with despair as these thoughts rushed through his mind. He had no desire to fight in this conflict. Arjuna had no choice but to turn to Lord Krishna for guidance and enlightenment after letting his bow slip from his grasp.

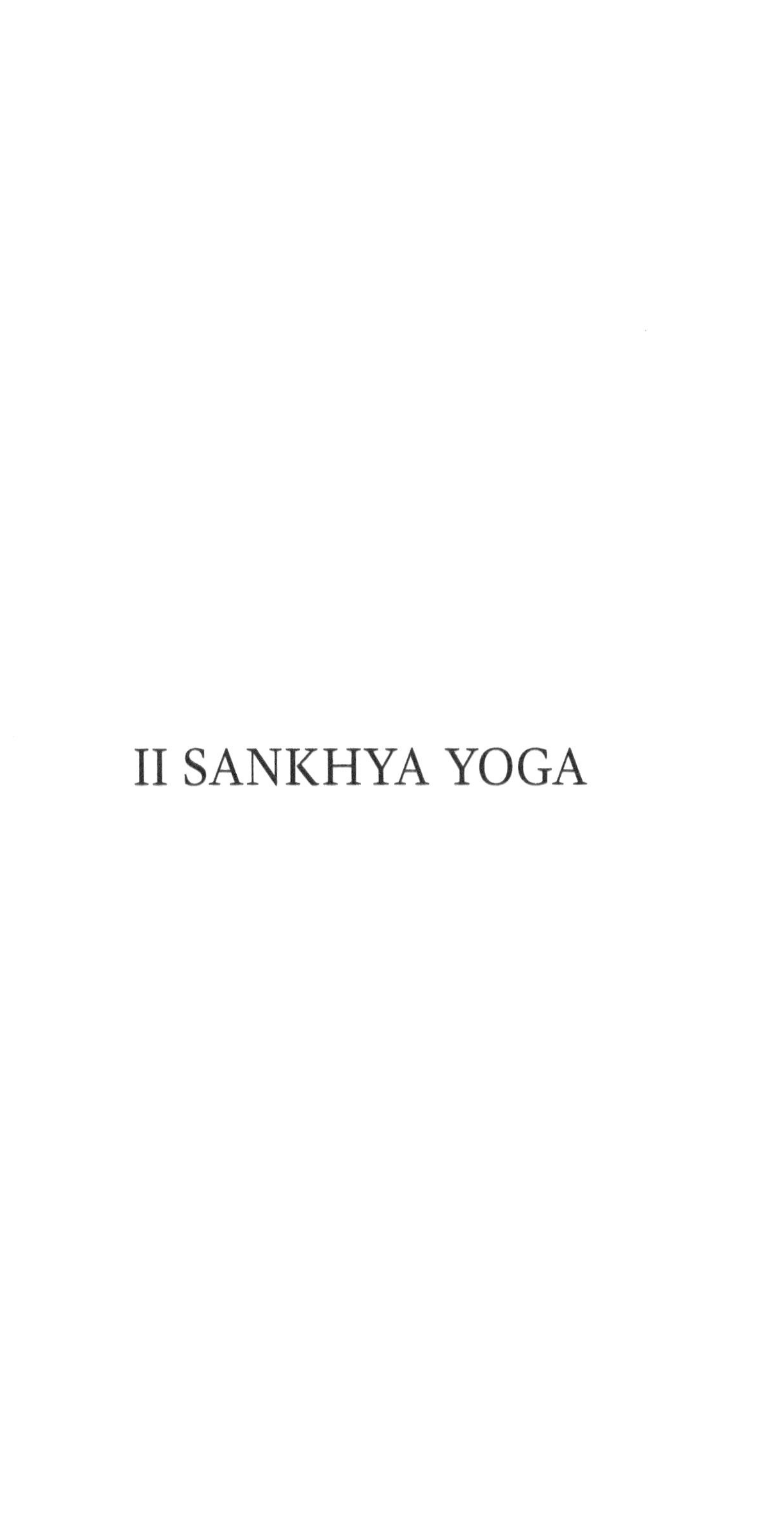

II SANKHYA YOGA

CHAPTER THREE

SECOND DISCLOSURE

Sanjaya explains Arjuna's agitation, which was caused by attachment and fear. Lord Krishna chastises him for his despair, which he attributes to Moha, or attachment, and encourages him to fight. Arjuna realises his helplessness after failing to persuade Sri Krishna with his seemingly wise thoughts, and surrenders himself completely to the Lord, seeking His guidance to resolve his mental conflict. The Lord takes pity on him and uses various methods to enlighten him. He explains to Arjuna the immutability of the Atman, which has no past, present, or future. Arjuna should not be sad because the Atman never dies. It cannot be cut, burned, or dried because it transcends the five elements of earth, water, fire, air, and ether. It is eternal and unchanging. Due to the contact of objects with the senses, everyone experiences conditions such as pleasure and pain, heat and cold. The nerves transmit sensations from the senses to the mind.

Like the tortoise, which withdraws all of its limbs within, one should be able to withdraw one's senses from objects. Only those who can be balanced in pleasure and pain, according to Krishna, are fit for immortality. People will be justified in condemning Arjuna's action as unworthy of a warrior if he refuses to fight and flees the battle, Krishna continues. After teaching Arjuna about the immortal nature of the Atman, Lord Krishna moves on to doing good without expecting anything in return. A man should not be concerned with the outcome of his actions, such as gain or loss, victory or defeat. These are in the Lord's hands. He should perform all actions with a balanced mind, calmly enduring the pairs of opposites that inevitably manifest during action, such as heat and cold, pleasure and pain. Arjuna is advised by Krishna to fight without the desire to gain or keep his kingdom. Arjuna is curious about the characteristics of a mentally stable man. Krishna tells him that such a person will have no desires at all. He is completely free of desires because he is content within, having realised the Self. Atman consciousness and desire abandonment are both simultaneous experiences. The Lord describes the various qualities of a Sthitaprajna (a stable-minded person). Adversity will have no effect on him, and he will be fearless and angry. He will accept things as they are and will not have any preferences. He will neither love nor hate the world.

A man with a stable mind will have complete control over his senses. The senses are strong, and they pull the mind outwards. As a result, one should look within and recognise God, who resides in the heart. Even when all sense-objects come to him, the Yogi, having achieved a stable mind, remains steadfast. He remains motionless and lives in eternal peace. Krishna concludes that being in the eternal Brahmic state permanently frees one from delusion. Even when one leaves this body at the end of life, one retains consciousness of one's identity with Brahman.

15

III THE YOGA OF ACTION

CHAPTER FOUR

THIRD DISCLOSURE

Sri Krishna taught Arjuna the imperishable nature of the Atman, which when realised would grant him the freedom of the Eternal, in order to remove Moha, or attachment, which was the sole cause of his delusion. As a result, Arjuna has doubts about the necessity of continuing to act even after attaining this state. Sri Krishna dispels his doubts by explaining that, despite realising oneness with the Eternal, one must act through the force of Prakriti, or Nature. He emphasises that perfection is attained not by ceasing to act, but by performing all actions as a divine offering imbued with non-attachment and sacrifice.

Sri Krishna explains to Arjuna that the man of God-vision does not need to take action because he has accomplished everything that needs to be accomplished. He can be completely immersed in the calm and unchanging Self. However, taking action for the greater good and mass education is unquestionably superior. As a result, action is required not only by those who have achieved perfection but also by those who are striving for perfection. Sri Krishna uses the example of Janaka, India's great sage-king, who continued to rule his kingdom even after realising God. The three qualities of Rajas, Tamas, and Sattwa make up Prakriti, or Nature. These three qualities and their functions are not the Atman. Man can only achieve perfection once he understands this fact. The Lord tells Arjuna that each person should do his or her duty in accordance with his or her nature, and that doing so in the right spirit of detachment will lead to perfection.

Arjuna poses the question of why people do things that cloud their minds and drag them down, as it were, by force. Sri Krishna responds that desire drives man to lose his discrimination and understanding, leading to wrongdoing. All evil actions stem from a desire for something. When desire is removed, the divine power manifests in all of its glory, and peace, bliss, light, and freedom are experienced.

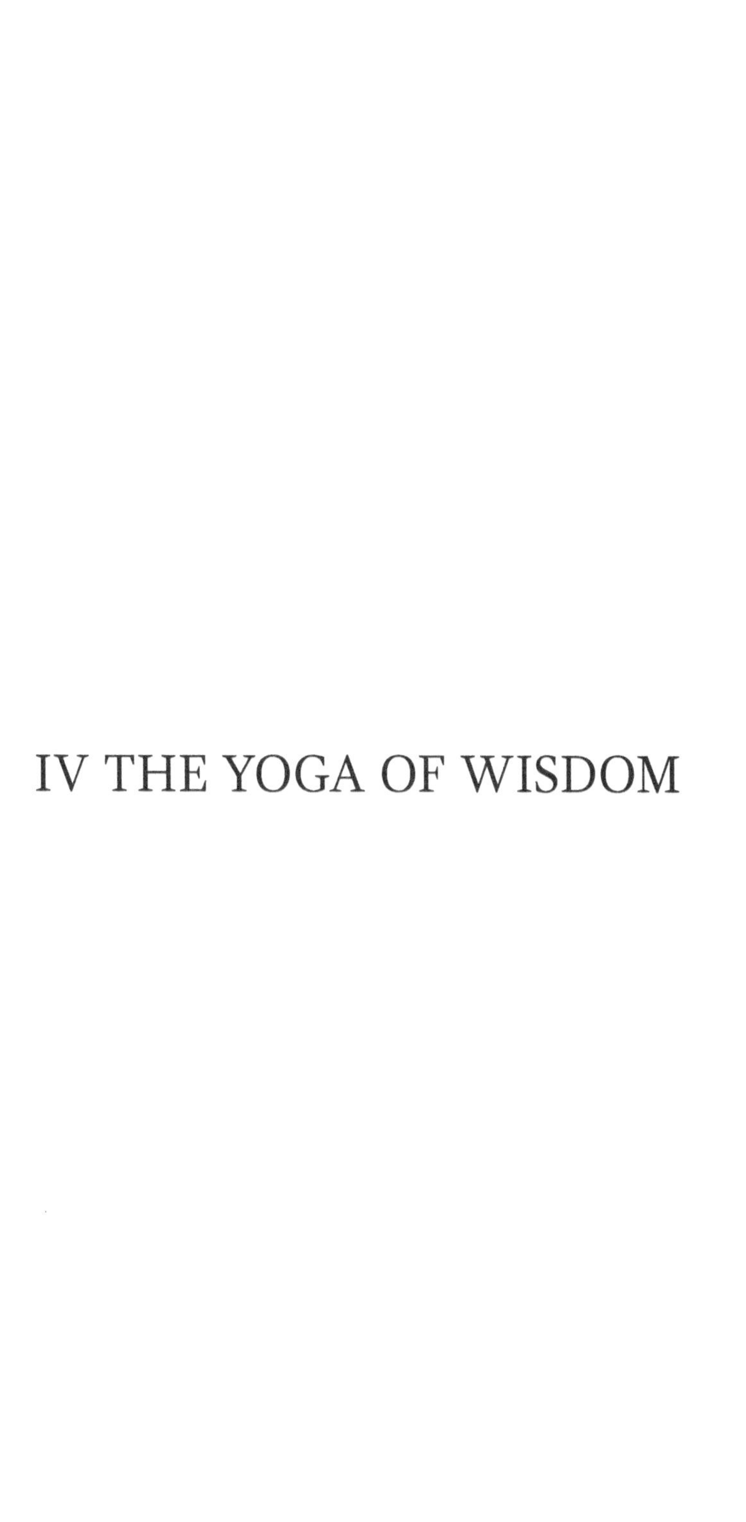# IV THE YOGA OF WISDOM

CHAPTER FIVE

FOURTH DISCLOSURE

Lord Krishna declares that He is born from generation to generation in order to uplift man and lead him to the Supreme. When unrighteousness is prevalent and the world is ruled by the forces of darkness, the Lord manifests Himself to destroy these adversarial forces and restore peace, order, and harmony. As a result, we see the appearance of the world's great saviours.

What is the Yogic secret to action? The Lord then proceeds to explain this to Arjuna. It is action in inaction if the mind is active with the idea of doership and egoism, even if one is not engaged in action. On the other hand, even if physically engaged in intense action, if the concept of agency is absent, if one believes Prakriti does everything, this is inaction in action. Even though he is constantly engaged in action, the liberated man is always calm and serene. He is unaffected by opposites such as happiness and sadness, success and failure. Rebirth is not an option for those in true union with the Lord. He becomes immortal. Only when one is free of attachment, fear, and anger, and thoroughly purified by the right knowledge, can such a union be achieved. The Lord accepts everyone's devotion, regardless of how they approach Him. Those on the path to God make various types of sacrifices. The mind is purified and led Godward through the practice of these sacrifices. There must also be a spirit of non-attachment to the results of actions here.

Sri Krishna recommends seeking divine wisdom at the feet of a liberated Guru, one who has realised the Truth. Such a sage should be approached with humility and devotion by the aspirant. God manifests Himself in the Guru's heart and instructs the disciple. The aspirant is no longer deluded by ignorance after receiving the Truth from the Guru through direct intuitive experience. The liberated aspirant sees the Self in all beings and the Self in all beings. All beings, from the Creator to a blade of grass, exist in his own Self and also in God, which he realises through internal experience or intuition. Arjuna receives the reassuring assurance that divine wisdom can free even the most depraved. When Self-knowledge dawns, all actions and their outcomes are consumed by the fire of that knowledge, just as fuel is consumed by fire. Actions are meaningless if there is no sense of egoism, no desire for the fruits of one's actions. They lose their effectiveness. To achieve divine wisdom, one must have unwavering faith and devotion. As a result, the most important qualification for a spiritual seeker is faith. The doubting mind is always led down the wrong path. Finally, faith bestows divine knowledge, eradicating ignorance once and for all.

Intellectual understanding alone does not lead to liberation. It cannot grant absolute peace and liberty. True knowledge dawns within and one attains liberation and freedom from all weaknesses and sins when one has achieved complete self-mastery and self-control when one has intense faith and devotion. Finally, the Lord emphasises that the soul that doubts will be destroyed. One cannot progress on the spiritual path without faith in oneself, the scriptures, and the words of the preceptor. Doubt is what keeps people from practising spiritual Sadhana and attaining the highest levels of knowledge and bliss. One's doubts are dispelled and divine knowledge manifests itself within by following the Guru's instructions and providing sincere service. The spiritual progress then accelerates.

V THE YOGA OF RENUNCIATION OF ACTION

CHAPTER SIX

FIFTH DISCLOSURE

Despite Sri Krishna's explicit instructions, Arjuna appears perplexed. He wants to know for sure whether the path of action or the path of renunciation of action is superior. Both paths, according to the Lord, lead to God's highest goal of realisation. The ultimate goal in both cases is to realise the Atman, but the Karma Yoga path is superior. In reality, there isn't much of a difference between the two. Krishna goes on to say that after the mind has been purified through selfless action, perfection can be attained and one can be established in the Atman. Although the intellect, mind, and senses are active, the Karma Yogi who is aware of the Atman and is constantly engaged in action knows that he does nothing. Everything is a spectator sport for him. He devotes all of his actions to the Lord, abandoning attachment and remaining pure and unaffected throughout. He completely surrenders himself to Divine Shakti. He is not born again because he has completely eradicated all desires, attachments, and the ego.

There is no rebirth for the sage who has realised Brahman and is always absorbed in It. Within and without, such a sage sees Brahman as the static and transcendent Brahman, and outside as the entire universe. He sees the one Self in all beings and creatures, including cows, elephants, dogs, and outcasts. He is eternally free of joy and sorrow, and he lives in peace and happiness. He does not rely on his senses to satisfy him. The pleasures of the senses, on the other hand, are pain generators. They are transient. Arjuna is reminded by Sri Krishna that desire is the root of all pain and suffering. It's the source of rage.

If the aspirant is to reach the Supreme, he must try to eliminate desire and anger. Finally, the Lord explains how to control the senses, mind, and intellect by focusing between the eyebrows and practising Pranayama. Liberation and perfect peace are attained by one who has perfect control of the outgoing senses and is free of desire, anger, and fear.

VI THE YOGA OF MEDITATION

CHAPTER SEVEN

SIXTH DISCLOSURE

Sri Krishna emphasises that a Yogi or Sannyasin is someone who has given up the fruits of their actions rather than the actions themselves. Purification of the mind occurs when actions are carried out without regard for the consequences. Only a pure mind, one devoid of desires, is capable of constant meditation on the Atman. Desire gives birth to the imagination, or Sankalpa, which propels the soul into action. As a result, no one can achieve permanent mental freedom and tranquillity without giving up desires.

The Higher Self must exert control over the lower self. The power of the higher Self must control all lower impulses of the body, mind, and senses. The Higher Self then becomes a friend. He who is united with God and has perfect control over his body, mind, and senses sees God in all objects and beings. He sees no distinction between gold and stone, between friends and enemies, or between the righteous and the unrighteous from within. He is in perfect harmony. Sri Krishna then goes on to give various tips on how to meditate effectively. The aspirant should choose a quiet location with little chance of being disturbed. He should sit in a comfortable posture, with his head, neck, and spine erect but not tense, in his meditation seat. By concentrating between the brows or on the tip of the nose, he should fix his purified mind on the Atman.

If one wants to be successful in meditation, one must practise Brahmacharya. The ability to concentrate is greatly enhanced by the conservation and transformation of vital fluid into spiritual energy. On the Godward path, fearlessness is also a necessary quality. It is trust in God's everlasting protection and grace. The aspirant should exercise moderation in his daily habits, such as eating, sleeping, and recreational activities. Extremes should be avoided because they obstruct meditation practice. The aspirant gradually transcends the senses and intellect and merges himself in the blissful Atman by living a life of such moderation and gathering all his forces and directing them towards meditation on the Atman.

He discovers that Atman's bliss is unrivalled and that there is no gain greater than the Self. The Yogi no longer descends into ignorance or delusion after achieving perfect union with the Self. He is no longer interested in sensual pleasures. Lord Krishna emphasises once more that the mind's concentration on the Atman should be like a constant flame in a windless place. This eventually leads to the Lord's vision in all beings and creatures. Arjuna is unsure whether it is even possible to focus the mind on the higher Self consistently, given that the mind's nature appears to be restless. Krishna assures him that with Vairagya (compassion) and consistent effort, the practice will succeed. Arjuna is curious about the fate of the aspirant who, despite his faith and sincerity, fails to realise the Supreme. Krishna assures him that the combined power of his Yogic practises will ensure him a better birth in the future, with better Sadhana conditions. The aspirant will then be compelled to continue his Yogic practises with increased vigour and faith, eventually achieving God-realisation.

Because the ascetics, men of book knowledge, and men of action have not transcended ignorance and merged in the Self, Krishna concludes that the Yogi—one who has attained union with the Supreme Lord—is superior to them.

VII THE YOGA OF WISDOM AND REALISATION

CHAPTER EIGHT

SEVENTH DISCLOSURE

Sri Krishna tells Arjuna that the redemptive and eternal aspects of the supreme Divinity must be realised. The Yogi who has reached the peak has learned everything there is to know. It is difficult to achieve complete union with the Lord. Only a small percentage of the world's population aspires to this union, and even fewer reach the pinnacle of spiritual realisation. The Lord has already described the all-pervading static and infinite state of His in detail. He then goes on to explain His manifestations as the universe and the power that drives them. These manifestations are referred to as His lower and higher Prakriti.

The five principles, mind, ego, and intellect, make up the lower Prakriti. The higher Prakriti is the life element that sustains, activates, and causes the universe's appearance and eventual dissolution.

Krishna claims that everything that exists is nothing more than Himself. He is the one who brought the universe and everything in it into existence. Everything is hung around Him like gem clusters on a string. He is the essence, substance, and foundation of all things, visible and invisible. He transcends everything as the actionless Self, despite the fact that everything is in Him. Sattwa, Rajas, and Tamas are the three Gunas or qualities that make up Prakriti, or Nature.

These characteristics deceive the soul, causing it to forget its true nature as one with God. Only the Lord's Grace can remove this delusion, which is known as Maya. Arjuna has been taught the highest form of devotion so far, which leads to union with God in both His static and dynamic aspects. Krishna informs him that there are other types of devotion that are inferior because they are performed for different reasons. The distressed, the seeker of divine wisdom, and those seeking wealth, as well as the wise, worship Him. The wise are the ones the Lord values the most. A devotee like this loves the Lord solely for the sake of pure love.Whatever form the disciple idolises, the Lord Himself is the ultimate goal. The Lord accepts such worship because He knows it is solely for Him.

VIII THE YOGA OF THE IMPERISHABLE BRAHMAN

CHAPTER NINE

EIGHTH DISCLOSURE

Lord Krishna explains how those who achieve Him will never have to return to this changeless world of sadness and grief. All beings, including gods, return to this material universe from their state of unmanifest being at the end of an age cycle. However, the Lord exists beyond this intangible being. The highest goal to be attained is that radiant, imperishable Divine Reality. The path to this highest blessed state is through our hearts' solitary worship. Even though there are favourable and unfavourable circumstances for departing from the physical existence and venturing forward, these circumstances are irrelevant if one consistently adheres to the Lord through strong commitment and belief. Everything is made noteworthy by remaining in tune with the Lord through pure love; if one can ever remain united with the Divine through deep devotion, constant remembrance, regular meditation, and continuous communion, all times, places, conditions, and situations become auspicious and blessed. This is the key to obtaining His Grace and living a forevermore unrestricted and joyous life.

Arjuna inquires of Lord Krishna well about the meanings of the various terms mentioned by Him. He wants to know who the Supreme Being is, what Karma or action He is referring to, and what this soul, the aspects, and the centre of all things within this human body mean. There is the Supreme Being—Brahman—beyond all things profound and unmanifest, beyond these identities and structures. He inhabits this body as the centre of everything, including ourselves (individual soul). We are spiritual beings residing in this body, supported by the Supreme Antaryamin, the Quiet Testimony. Nature, or Prakriti, is a being associated with the elements. Praise, worship, and offerings to the gods performed with faith and devotion result in blessings. The key to reaching the Divine Being and thus forever escaping birth and death, as well as the aches and miseries of this earthly existence, is to exercise unchanging remembrance of the Lord at all times, in all places, and even in the midst of one's daily activities. If one practises such steady remembrance through regular daily Sadhana, he will be rooted in His devotion even after he has passed away from this body. As a result of his departure, he will transcend darkness and enslavement and enter the world of eternal paradise.

It is necessary to practise self-control. The senses must be trained and gradually removed from external stimuli. By uttering Om or any other Divine Name, the mind should be focused on God. The Lord is easily accessible through such consistent daily practice.

IX THE YOGA OF THE KINGLY SCIENCE & THE KINGLY SECRET

CHAPTER TEN

NINTH DISCLOSURE

Krishna declares to Arjuna the self governing wisdom and supreme key that can only be known through direct experience after observing that he is an eligible applicant and bestowed with devotion. He goes on to say that without trust in this wisdom, man will never reach God and will be reborn to suffer. The Lord now goes on to describe Himself as the eternal, all-encompassing Truth. He is both the invisible and the visible. He pervades the entire universe. He creates all, upholds it all, and soaks up it all into Himself when it all comes to an end. When the next existence begins, he unfolds them again. All beings who are unaware of this knowledge are helpless victims of the birth and death cycle.

The Lord exists as a quiet testimony, unharmed and detached, in the midst of the universe's formation, retention, and disintegration. His Cosmic Prakriti is directed, sustained, and supervised by Him alone.

Ignorant people cannot recognise the Lord in someone who has discovered Him. The nature of these cruel beings is that of demons, despite their human appearance. The God-realized Mahatma, on the other hand, is a wise man who recognises God in all beings and creatures. In all names and forms, he sees the essential connection of existence.

All who take asylum in the Lord are assured of god's guidance. Whatever route a devotee takes, he will eventually reach Him. He is the ultimate goal of all spiritual disciplines. Sri Krishna reinforces that devotion is at the heart of all spiritual disciplines. If this supreme value is found, the devotee is set free from his or her enslavement. The Lord looks at the motivation and level of devotion. Even for the most depraved and devious man can reach the Lord if he makes a drastic turn toward righteousness and truth. Regardless of one's profession, if one seeks the Lord sincerely and with loving devotion, one can find Him.The most important thing is to resolve one's thoughts on the Lord and devote one's body, mind, actions, emotions, and will to Him.

X THE YOGA OF THE DIVINE GLORIES

CHAPTER ELEVEN

TENTH DISCLOSURE

Even the Devas and evolved human souls, Krishna tells Arjuna, are unable to comprehend how He manifests Oneself as the multiverse and all of its embodiments. He then goes on to explain the different aspects that people exhibit as a result of their Karmas. All of these characteristics—wisdom, truth, fulfilment, and so on—come from Him.

True worshipers of the Divine are completely consumed by Him. They have entirely conceded to Him, and He has granted them the power of unequal treatment, the bias that will lead them from the unreal to the real. Krishna declares categorically that misconceptions is eliminated and understanding is acquired solely through God's intervention.

XI THE YOGA OF THE VISION OF THE COSMIC FORM

CHAPTER TWELVE

ELEVENTH DISCLOSURE

Arjuna's doubts have been dismissed by a simple comprehension of the nature of the Atman, as well as the source and damage of all created things, and he is now ready to witness the Cosmic Vision. Krishna bestows on Arjuna the godly vision, allowing him to see the Creator as the vast Cosmic Incarnation. The vision is simultaneously all-encompassing and concurrent. Arjuna sees the Lord as the infinite cosmos from every angle. All of the created realms, gods, beings, creatures, and things are revealed to be the Lord's one massive body. Arjuna also notices that the Lord's all-powerful power has set in motion and is controlling the celestial theatrics. In all things and deeds, good and bad, His Will alone reigns supreme. The Lord obliges him to fight, despite the fact that he is only a visible cause of his foes' destruction.

Arjuna is terrified, unable to bear the tension of the transient flow of awareness. He begs the Lord to return to His original form. Krishna highlights that this vision cannot be attained through penance, research, compromises, or charitable acts. The only way to gain access to His long term vision is through supreme loyalty.

XII THE YOGA OF DEVOTION

CHAPTER THIRTEEN

TWELFTH DISCLOSURE

According to the twelfth discourse, the path of worship is easier than the path of wisdom. The aspirant on this path worships God in His Supreme Character's Celestial Version. He cultivates a special bond with Him, adores Him, recognises Him, and sings His praises. As a result, he achieves union with the Lord, not only in His formless aspect, but also as the manifest universe. The path of wisdom, in which the seeker meditates on the formless Brahman, is more difficult because it requires the person to give up his connection to the body from the start. He must be uninterested in the worldly things.

How can devotion be practised? Arjuna is told by Krishna to focus his entire mind on Him. The mind should be revived to the Lord as often as it drifts. If concentration is difficult, he should devote all of his acts to Him, believing that everything is activated by His power. If this is also further than his abilities, he should offer all of his acts to the Lord, renouncing his desire for the fruits of his labours. He should seek refuge in Him completely. The devotee who completely bows down to the Lord finds complete peace.

The Lord goes on to explain the characteristics of a true worshipper. He has no attachments to anything, and he has no aversions to anything. In any situation, he has a stable mind. He is not agitated by the events of the world, nor does he cause others to be agitated. He has no desires and finds comfort in the Lord within him. He sees fairness everywhere, unaffected by sadness, anxiety, or dignity or disrespect. He is completely content because he has given God his entire being.

XIII THE YOGA OF DISTINCTION BETWEEN THE FIELD & THE KNOWER OF THE FIELD

CHAPTER FOURTEEN

THIRTEENTH DISCLOSURE

We have one of the most meaningful, enlightening, empowering, and mythic segments of the Bhagavad Gita in this discourse. The Lord gives us a wonderful glimpse into the human personality. It's man's metaphysics, the unknown. This discussion centres on the immortal Soul and its physical manifestation. The supreme transcendental Spirit, which is the eternal substratum beyond both, is also magnificently described. The one who understands the Supreme Reality is instantly set free. The real wisdom, according to the glorious Lord, is the expertise of the Field and the Knower of the Field. This ultimate and best understanding bestows heavenly wisdom and spiritual enlightenment, resulting in divine bliss. The Field is this body. The Knower of the Field is the Immortal Soul (yourself), who resides in the body. Indeed, it is the Supreme Being who has projected Himself into this body and adopted the form of this Perceiver of the Field. That is the identity of this self. As a result, Lord Krishna clarifies the mystery of the individual soul residing in this mortal body. This wisdom is the central theme of all the scriptures and the best scholarly writings. The Field is made up of the five elements, the ego, mind, intellect, 10 organs, desire and aversion, and other components. Following that is a beautiful summary of what true knowledge is. The Supreme Soul's proclamation follows, and awareness of it guarantees us immortality. That Absolute Being is the single global Essence that exists in all places. It penetrates everything. It glows from the depths of our hearts; it is everything; it is the one sorcerer, the observer, the counselor, the preserver, the perceiver, and the Lord of all.

In the course of life, one who understands this wonder is not constrained by activity. We cannot harm anyone when we recognise the divine Presence that dwells in all beings. To approach the Self, Krishna invites us to recognise and realize the distinction between the Subject and the Researcher of the Field . This is the essence and the lesson of this enlightening talk.

XIV THE YOGA OF THE DIVISION OF THE THREE GUNAS

FOURTEENTH DISCLOSURE

This discourse now imparts insight into the three universal aspects of Gunas, namely Sattwa, Rajas, and Tamas. The understanding of these three Gunas, which govern the entire cosmos and all beings, is critical to everyone's advancement and enjoyment in life. Without this understanding, one will be bound by grief for the rest of one's life. We hold the key to success in both the earthly and spiritual realms in this understanding. As a result, this priceless knowledge should be acquired. These three traits, according to Lord Krishna, make up Cosmic Nature. This Cosmic Nature is the basic root and foundation of everything in the universe. As a result, everything created is prone to their impact and unstoppable power. These three properties found in Cosmic Nature also bind the individual soul to the body. The Supreme Being creates with the aid of His Prakriti (Nature), which is equipped with these three attributes. Sattwa is the finest of the three virtues. It is unadulterated. It promotes happiness, wisdom, and illumination. Rajas' second attribute is passion, which manifests itself as extreme attachment and avarice. It brings sadness and pain. The third, Tamas, is the most dangerous of them all. It is caused by ignorance and manifests as gloom, sluggishness, and deception. Krishna advises us to work hard to eliminate Tamas from our origins. We must manage and regulate Rajas, and by keeping them in check, we may properly direct their force toward beneficial tasks. Sattwa must be carefully nurtured, developed, and preserved if we are to achieve immortality. Of course, the realised sage transcends all of these attributes, for, while Sattwa is what allows him to realize Divinity, it is the same quality that will confine him if he is devoted to it.

The seeker should be aware of the signs and signals of their involvement in his persona, as well as the subtle workings of these entities. Only then will he be able to move freely and smoothly in all aspects of his life, secular and spiritual. From the ninth through the eighteenth verses of this speech, Lord Krishna explains to us this vital subject. He claims that anyone who climbs above all three Gunas via spiritual activities achieves immortality and is free of birth, death, old age, and grief. In response to Arjuna's enquiry, the blessed Lord reveals the characteristics of someone who has climbed well above three Gunas. He claims that if one idolises Him with complete devotion all of the time, one will have the ultimate heavenly experience, as well as ultimate peace and blessings.

XV THE YOGA OF THE SUPREME SPIRIT

CHAPTER SIXTEEN

FIFTEENTH DISCLOSURE

"Yoga of the Supreme Person," is the title of this discourse. Here, Lord Krishna describes the sole source of this observable phenomenal cosmos, from which all things have sprung forth, similar to a large tree with all its grounds, stem, arms, buds, foliage, flowers, and fruits that spring out upon the earth, which supports and roots the tree. Sri Krishna asserts that the Ultimate Being is the basis of all existing, and compares the world to an upright tree whose roots are in Absolute Brahman and whose extending branches and foliage represent all the elements and factors that go into making up this creation of diverse manifestations. This is a mystery "Tree" that is difficult to comprehend, as it is a creation of His unfathomable Maya power, and hence has a wonderful, seeming appearance but no actual existence. Beyond Maya is the one who truly comprehends the natural order of this Samsara Tree. Becoming entrapped in it is being attached to it. Dispassion and non-attachment are the most effective weapons for overcoming this Samsara or earthly existence. the Lord explains how to transcend this visible Samsara and achieve supreme, imperishable status, after which one is free of the need to return to this mortal world of agony and death.

Lord Krishna also explains the beautiful wonder of His Being in this universe, as well as the tremendous role He plays in supporting everything. Our Lord declares that the unique soul in each body is a piece of Him manifesting here. Beyond the self, He is the sanctifying grace. He is the sun, moon, and fire's innate brilliance. He is present in the earth as the feeding ingredient. All beings have an inner witness in them. Even above Vedic knowledge, He is the greatest Knower. He is the radiant One who transcends simultaneously this perishable phenomenal world and the indestructible individual soul that is a portion of His eternal essence. He is known as the Ultimate Being both in this world and in the Vedas because He is beyond perishable substance and incomparable to the immortal soul.

XVI THE YOGA OF THE DIVISION BETWEEN THE DIVINE AND THE DEMONIACAL

CHAPTER SEVENTEEN

SIXTEENTH DISCLOSURE

This discourse is significant and instructional for anyone who wants to be happy, prosperous, and fortunate, but especially for seekers who want to be successful in their spiritual lives. Lord Krishna emphasises the close relationship between morals and spiritual practices, between a virtuous path and God-realization and freedom, in this verse. The Lord distinguishes between godly and demoniacal (undivine) attributes, advising us to eliminate the latter and develop the former. What kind of environment should one cultivate? What are the rules of conduct? If one wishes to reach God and experience divine happiness, how should one live and act? These questions were addressed with utmost precision and certainty. Pure divine traits promote serenity and liberation, while undivine traits lead to enslavement. Purity, good deeds, and truth are necessary for spiritual advancement and even a decent life here. Man deteriorates into such a creature of hideous personality and harsh actions, sinking into darkness, lacking of holiness, good conduct, and honesty, and having no confidence in God or a greater Reality beyond this visible world. Such a guy becomes his own worst enemy, destroying both others' and his own happiness. His existence ends in agony and humiliation as he is enslaved by endless impulses and needs, a slave of carnal desires, and harassed by a thousand cares. This terrible fate is caused by haughtiness, arrogance, and egoism. As a result, a smart person who wants to succeed must eliminate vice and embrace virtue.

Three gateways lead to damnation in this world: the portals of passion, rage, and greed. When these three attributes are released, one can achieve salvation and reach the highest objective, which is God. As a result, the sacred books wisely explain the correct path of pure, ethical existence. As a result, one should obey the sacred books' wishes for his well-being and be directed in his activities by their noble principles.

XVII THE YOGA OF THE DIVISION OF THE THREEFOLD FAITH

CHAPTER EIGHTEEN

SEVENTEENTH DISCLOSURE

The "Yoga of the Division of the Three Kinds of Faith" is the label assigned to this discourse. "What about those who, while disregarding scriptural injunctions, do they worship with faith?" asks Arjuna in response to Lord Krishna's final and concluding counsel in the preceding speech. The Lord responds by saying that such men's faith could be Sattwic, Rajasic, or Tamasic, depending on whether they violate the scriptures' injunctions.

This would be consistent with the person's fundamental nature. In turn, as the type of faith develops, so does the man's nature. As a result, in all things such as commitment, devotion, generosity, repentance, and so on, these attributes are represented in harmony with the person's beliefs. They produce effects in proportion to the doer's faith quality. These activities, when performed with correct faith, result in highest blessing. All of these actions become unproductive and pointless when accomplished with no faith.

XVIII THE YOGA OF LIBERATION BY RENUNCIATION

CHAPTER NINETEEN

EIGHTEENTH DISCLOSURE

The eighteenth discourse, which concludes Lord Krishna's holy discourse, summarises the preceding chapters of the Gita in many aspects. It summarises a number of key themes discussed in prior discussions. You may see the end consequence or effect of the Lord's lecture to Arjuna here. Arjuna's complete despair and breakdown are completely addressed in victorious conscience, power, and brave resoluteness. Its core message emerges as a guarantee that by rejecting egoism and attachment and surrendering every craving for greed, and self-benefit, one can fit for the ultimate freedom in and through the accomplishment of one's separate obligations in life. You receive the Lord's Grace and attain the everlasting One by considering the achievement of your obligations as worship dedicated to God. This debate begins with Arjuna's query about what constitutes authentic Sannyasa and true renunciation. In response to this vital question, the beloved Lord clarifies that true Sannyasa or renunciation is abstaining from selfish activities, and even more so, abstaining from the urge or appetite for the results of any activity. We are plainly taught that selfless and moral behaviours, as well as actions that benefit others, should not be neglected. You must engage yourself in such activities while avoiding attachment and greed. Giving up pride and passion while executing rightful tasks is authentic and proper renouncing. Sattwic Tyaga is the name for this. We have no strong feelings for either unpleasant or joyful actions. Because you cannot abandon all action, true renunciation is defined as the renunciation of egoism, greed, and commitment in your activities. Karma does not grow or hold someone who has reached this level of inner abstinence.

God must be made the sole focus of one's life, according to the holy command. This is the central message of the Gita. The basic message of its teaching is this. This is the only way to ensure your safety here. Sanjaya ends his story by asserting that when there is such obedience as Arjuna's, and such eagerness to follow in the holy precepts, it would undoubtedly be prosperity, triumph, glory, and all blessings.

www.ingramcontent.com/pod-product-compliance
Lightning Source LLC
Chambersburg PA
CBHW031316130726
47988CB00007B/2853